SERVANT ADVISORSHIP™

*The New Approach for Advisors Who Want
to Grow, Serve and Live with Excellence*

Kristopher Bonocore

It's not about you...

To my daughter, Madison, for motivating me with your unbendable confidence and infectious energy.

To my son, Ethan, for inspiring me with your intense focus and unwavering determination.

To my wife, Julie, for endearing me with your heartwarming compassion and support.

You all teach me so much every day. I am forever grateful.

Table of Contents

Calling Those Who Seek Excellence 7

Let's Get Real: The Preface 9

Summary of a Servant Advisor™ 15

Part One | My Story 23

Hellooooo Julie! 33

Opportunity and Tunnel Vision 42

The Role of Relentless Determination 46

What's Your Story? 63

Part Two | Walking the Walk 66

Part Three | Seeing is Believing 73

Vision and Value 78

Case Study: New Belgium Brewery 81

The Psychology of Visions 85

Manifestation's Role in Vision 97

Part Four | Seven Core Tenets 104

Tenet One: Be Understanding 107

Tenet Two: Be Selfless 111

Tenet Three: Be Accountable 115

Tenet Four: Be Influential 118

Tenet Five: Be Honorable...121

Tenet Six: Be Enthusiastic...124

Tenet Seven: Be Focused...127

Are You The Next Servant Advisor™?........................129

The Need for the Best Advisor Network 132

About Kristopher Bonocore...135

Acknowledgements...137

Contact Best Advisor Network 139

Appendix..140

Calling Those Who Seek Excellence

Best Advisor Network isn't for just anyone. It's for those willing to take the responsibility of being an Advisor to the next level. Not all are up to the task, much less the challenge. It's up to you to determine if you are or not.

Advisors in our network become Servant Advisors™ and benefit in two primary ways:

1. Become a world-class Advisor by leveraging the framework given to become a stand-out Advisor in their communities.
2. Make more confident decisions by using our consulting, coaching, and mentoring services.

Not everyone who claims the title of Advisor is cut out for this. It takes a perpetual commitment to the heart, soul, and intent of the Servant Advisor concept. There is no wearing this hat at work and then tossing it out the window on the way home. It's always on and it's legitimately you – on good days, on bad days, and during all the other crap that falls in between.

Clients always need steady and assured guidance from their Advisor. The best of you should be offered to them and nothing less should be acceptable.

Taking care of clients is first, always. You're the cart and the client is the horse. Get the idea? How can I best serve YOU?

I'm obsessed with creating Servant Advisors so I want to know the #1 question on your mind. Email me here: theservantadvisor@gmail.com

8

Let's Get Real: The Preface

I'm at a time in my life and career where writing a book isn't really a negotiable. Equally, our industry is at a time when change is needed. Clients will not continue to endure shallow, transactional relationships – nor should they. A unified effort to improve the way in which clients receive service and advice is now expected.

What I have learned and how I've put this knowledge into motion has guided me to this Servant Advisor™ philosophy. There's a bit of vanity involved in the desire to write a book, I suppose, but that's not my angle or my motivator. I'm the first one to admit that if I'd written a book when I first thought of it, it would have been a series of stories, thoughts, and ideas to "help" others, but it would have missed the mark. Think of a drawn arrow being released from the bow right when a strong gust of wind comes along – an epic miss happens a second later.

To become the master archer for these situations, you've got to have a few experiences. I've had these, and then some. Even shot myself in the foot with my own arrow a time or two.

Servant Advisorship™ is here to make an impact, create a movement. Whether you want to be a part of it or not is out of my control. It's not perfected, but if I said it were you shouldn't believe me. What I have chosen to share does work. I've lived it and for those of us in a competitive industry such as this, we know how important it is to deliver what our clients need most. This philosophy does this, which is why I am sharing it with my brothers and sisters of the Advisor community.

Look, I realize nobody has the time and desire to dive into complex topics. Life is already complicated enough at times, even for those of us who understand the financial services industry. So, this book is simple, nothing earth-shattering. I think of it more as a damn good way to live life, both at work and outside of work.

My journey has been defined.

And, yes, I am hoping you fit the bill to come along for the experience. It is one worth having.

ABBA had a dream and I have a vision. (That's the former DJ in me coming out.)

This gives you a glimpse of the results, which are the start of a bigger process, a handful of the best practices, crafted from experiences and results alike.

The financial services industry has treated me well, but I've put in my time to also be an asset to it. I've met and forged lifelong relationships with incredible clients, friends, mentors, and colleagues. I've learned so much and have barely scratched the surface. I've had remarkable people work for me and with me, and I've also worked for world-class leaders. All this motivates me to no end. It's exciting and it's what revs my engine. This is a non-negotiable if you're going to be in a competitive industry such as this and desire a chance to deliver what your clients need most.

I should caution you with this question: Are you ready to "learn it all?" If you are, let me know where you find a place to do that. I'm interested in joining you on *that* journey. In this moment, it's about knowing just a little bit more. How? The answer is, I've packaged and simplified what I've learned and experienced so that the Advisor community can deliver excellence to their clients. It's time to discover if you can be a Servant Advisor and make a difference in the lives of clients. Or do you want to be another Advisor with a fancy title?

If I would have had a committed adult who helped me figure this all out as a kid, they would have said something like, "The best work you do is work you do for others." Unfortunately, I didn't, so I had to learn it on my own. Sometimes it's better that way.

This book is filled with perspectives, observations, best practices, snippets of thought, and philosophies I've used as an Advisor and as an Advisor Leader. These insights have helped me grow businesses, build practices, and change lives. If you'd like to grow your business and are sick of looking at an endless plateau, consider thinking outside your box and let's talk.

Visit www.theservantadvisor.com or email me directly at theservantadvisor@gmail.com.

The name I have given to all this is Servant Advisorship. It's not about being perfect; it's about doing something better. Not bigger. Better. Our industry needs a refresher – a reminder of why we all started as Advisors. Servant Advisorship offers a new path. There exists a world of potential in genuinely improving our clients' lives, experiences, and relationships. This new world is very achievable. I've done it in my own microcosm, and now I want to share how you can too. In some ways, I'm naming and packaging what many great

Advisors have always done. The package is new, but not necessarily the content. Coca–Cola® made drinking cola into an experience. There are some good sodas out there – some taste even better than Coca-Cola. Regardless, that company has created a way to make us think of their name first when we hear the word "soda." Similarly, Servant Advisorship has never been done before and ultimately helps give clients something they can't get anywhere else.

You may have done some of these things throughout your career, or even do them in your practice today, but have yet to create a system with all of it together. I've done this, I've created it. I've grown a practice to $165 million in assets under management. I've helped thousands of clients create a path to financial success. I've led teams of Advisors to massive success. I didn't do any of this alone and I am forever grateful for the people who helped me along the way, but it did take me 40 years to figure it all out...and I'm still learning. I want you to get through this quicker than 40 years.

I've been observing myself all these years and now I'm going to share it with you. Why? Because I care about Advisors and I care about clients. I believe that if Advisors get what they need, then clients get what they need. Be careful not to confuse getting what they need with getting what they want. These are often very different things.

So here you have it…(half) a lifetime of wisdom and experiences broken down into key components to help you serve your clients better. By default, you'll find your personal life can get a bit better too. I've made plenty of mistakes there but, equally, I have plenty of triumphs (miraculous victories) to share also.

Let's journey, together.

Summary of a Servant Advisor™

"Where there is not community, trust, respect, ethical behavior are difficult for the young to learn and for the old to maintain."

- Robert K. Greenleaf, *The Servant as Leader*

Advisors and future Advisors, this is for you.

What is a Servant Advisor™? My inspiration for this term and philosophy comes from a book written by Robert Greenleaf in 1977 called *Servant Leadership: A journey into the nature of legitimate power and greatness*. This book's ideas had an immense impact on me about the value of a relationship between a leader (boss, Advisor, etc.) and those they serve. Over 40 years later, Servant Leadership is now widely adopted throughout the business world. Simply stated, the philosophy encourages leaders to serve their people. Servant Advisorship™ is not wildly different but takes it one step further, encouraging Advisors to serve their clients. You got that right. Advisors are the servants, not ones to be served by those lower than them on the employee totem pole.

I wondered, *how powerful would it be to evolve into a Servant Advisor?* It's a good question to ponder if you really want to make a difference in the lives of your clients. Other peoples' legacies and livelihoods depend on you. Big pressure!

Advisors should focus on the client first, rather than the product, commission, or so on. It starts with customer service and client management skills, but that only scratches the surface. The way you approach everything – EVERYTHING – is impacted by your values and vision.

But what about money, Kris? I need to make a living. If you thought this just now, you are not alone. I'd never suggest earning an income is not important. Money is a great tool for surviving and experiencing great things. Money can also lead you toward the cesspool of life if your values and the scope of your vision aren't strong, guiding forces.

I'm an Advisor who has put money first before. If you are currently an Advisor, the odds are good you have too. This is flawed. You know when it happens because you no longer experience personal joy in your work. "Let's get to work!" becomes "another day at the office..." Now nobody is serving anybody.

Your clients' best interests being served is a winning scenario for you. You can't lose (even despite yourself).

Advisors working for the wrong reasons is a disaster. A lack of a consistent belief system creates chaos for clients. They deserve better than that. They should trust you for a reason, not just because they need you. And that game will be up when they realize they maybe do not need you at all.

Advisors needs to deliver a better experience to clients in an authentic way. I've trained countless Advisors on this, have dived into this from the corporate level, and, most importantly (not to mention what I love best), have been the boots on the ground, a trusted Advisor to thousands of clients. Out of everything I've done and the success I've had, being an Advisor is where I've enjoyed the most rewarding experience.

Understanding what an Advisor really needs to provide for a client is necessary, unavoidable. If there were a recipe, it would be the 7 Core Tenets, combined with having a roadmap, that will be shared later in this book. Advisors can be okay or even good when missing an ingredient or two, but they can't be great. Clients have saved all their lives and will make one of the most important decisions of their life when choosing an Advisor. If their Advisor is average, it will limit other parts of their lives to being just average.

Clients' lives change for the better when they're confident their needs are being met first – that they take priority over their Advisor's or their Advisor's firm's needs. By nature, this is serving someone's needs well. It's not about you, as the Advisor.

It all comes down to benefit. Everyone likes to know they benefit. We're selfish by nature but for some things, we must be selfish – our survival and well-being often depend on it.

Believe in what's best for your clients.

Know you can deliver it.

Be all in, not just a half-assed player in the game.

Make an impact. Make a difference.

Promoting this type of culture for people who rely on an Advisor is important to me. Can we work together to create a massive wave of principled, servant-minded Advisors? If we don't, lives will be negatively impacted. Don't let the number of Advisors who really aren't committed to the entire scope of client service be the norm for our profession.

I challenge you to be better than that.

This book is broken into four main sections:

Part One | My Story
Why is it important for you to know about me? My life has been raw and interesting from the time I was a child up to the present. Everything that has happened has formed me, and even the lousiest aspects of it all have helped me stumble upon the key qualities that have led to my success. Similar experiences can lead to your success as well, so prepare to be uncomfortable. You're about to bust free from restrictions and confining ideals that do not work.

I challenge you to take the worst crap that has been flung your way and use it to your advantage. Instead of holding you back, it's catapulting you forward. A Servant Advisor does this, whether with a bit of fear or fearlessly.

Part Two | Walking the Walk
Just as the great Robert Greenleaf focused on Servant Leadership and how it serves people, you are at a point where you MUST KNOW what is

involved with transforming your business practices into something more meaningful than just the boring term "Advisor." Being a Servant Advisor means something – it's not a title just given; it's earned. We are not entitled to anything in this business.

Part Three | Seeing is Believing

If you don't know the differences between dreams, goals, and visions, you really don't know if you're doing anything right. I know a thing or two about vision, enough to realize it's misunderstood by most people. Some think they know, but they're off track. Getting off track is tricky. It can be a slow derailment or, bam! You're suddenly paralyzed and ineffective. I've been there. I can't wait to dive into this with you because it takes you from the concept of being a Servant Advisor to actually jumping in and showing your clients how awesome your spirit of service is to their well-being.

Part Four | 7 Core Tenets – The Foundation

I love (and live) these. I could not have done what I've done without them. When you understand these, serious shifts will take place. Knock you off your old way of thinking, jar your actions into the right direction. It's massive stuff that will lead to massive action. The 7 Core Tenets, when combined with vision and determination, bring it all together.

This is where change happens and no one may be able to define it specifically, but they feel it. Clients trust the process with you more, and you know that they do. Relationships strengthen, you know your clients better and get what their lives are about. It becomes more than casual chit-chat before you shove a predetermined product down their throat. Solutions should NEVER be predetermined.

Furthermore, the 7 Core Tenets are like a puzzle – if one piece is missing, it just does not work. All this together forms the recipe that creates a Servant Advisor. Your heart and mind shift in big ways. You sense it and you love it. I mean, really love it, like you enjoy doing your favorite activity. It's as sweet as golfing under par, winning your marathon race division, or enjoying your favorite glass of wine in a pristine setting that reminds you how great this world is. It's all that – and more.

Clients have inherent needs and you have certain responsibilities as the person who is influencing their lives. Service comes in many forms and it is centered on what "they," the client, wants:

- They want their calls returned promptly.
- They want you to do what you've promised.
- They want you to fulfill your marketing suggestions.

- They want to be listened to and heard.
- They want their questions answered.
- They want their fears quelled.
- They want their needs met.

All these things are important. There is one thing even more important that "they" want from you, and that's a trusting relationship. Trust doesn't exist simply because someone boisterously says they're trustworthy. Because I've got news for you: If you must tell someone you're trustworthy, you are in the midst of an epic fail. Trust is formed through demonstrating enough that you reveal you are trustworthy.

We need our clients and our clients need us. The principles of Servant Advisorship are a better groundwork for serving clients' needs.

It's time to step up to the plate and embrace this philosophy, this opportunity.

We don't hesitate to take or charge fees for our services, so why should we hesitate to make every client request a priority?

Part One | My Story

"Your life story is a gift, and it should be treated as such."

- Emily V. Gordon

You're about to read a chapter that is anything but a sweet story of growing up into your own. Yes, it's that kind of story.

If you're anything like me, you recognize how jarring, true stories lead to the most growth. Hearing someone whose story is worse than yours automatically makes you think, *if that guy can make it through what has happened to him, I don't have anything to complain about.*

We all have first memories from childhood. Ice cream, special toys, images of our parents, time spent together. This is all common. Take a moment to picture it and enjoy the reflection. It feels good, right?

Well, I could sit here for a day and can only get glimpses of good times rolling in my mind from when I was a kid. My life was not common, and those things generally didn't exist for me.

But here's one memory I managed to put together for you, just to give you an idea...

I was four years old, sitting on the floor and staring at the cheap, dingy, marked-up door of my mom's apartment. First there was a loud bang. Then a bunch of yelling.

Even as a toddler, I knew something bad was about to happen. I couldn't escape the thought any more than I could escape the shock of the cops kicking in the door a bit later.

I knew my alphabet enough to recite "DEA." Of course, I had no idea what DEA was at the time. Their visit resulted in my mom being busted for possession and dealing of cocaine. Oh, I almost forgot, she was also concealing a loaded weapon without a license. Turns out this gun was used years earlier in the robbery of a convenience store.

Twenty years later, my mom died of an overdose on Christmas Day.

Fast-forward another ten years, and my brother died of liver failure. He had contracted Hepatitis C from

Mom at birth. Nurture, combined with nature, had taken my brother.

I will never have an opportunity to understand my mom in any capacity. I never knew her free of addiction or affliction. My legal name is Kristopher Levin Kane Bonocore. Kristopher, courtesy of my mother's admiration for Kris Kristofferson. Levin, my elusive biological father's name. Kane, my mom's maiden name. Bonocore, my mom's first husband's surname. He adopted me, then overdosed not long after, leaving my mom nine months pregnant with her second child, my brother Michael.

There was another marriage and two more children, including the brother who passed from liver failure.

I've watched my mother try killing herself with, yes, razor blades on several occasions. Not a pretty sight.

I've witnessed my mother doing drugs and dealing drugs. I saw her handcuffed, thrown in jail and sent to nine drug rehab centers, forcing my brother and me to live with family members for periods of time.

I've also witnessed violent fights involving my mother.

I've witnessed and experienced things I may never share.

The dreamier version of my mom who I wish I would have had a chance to know was the smart, beautiful, ambitious, athletic type that, everyone reminded her, existed once upon a time. I rarely saw a glimpse of that woman. I'm pretty sure I would have liked her if I had. I loved my mom, but I did not like her very much. I would have been equally safe as a kid if I was playing in front of an open window with scissors and a loaded gun. Really.

Somehow, Mom went from all those "golden accolades" to becoming a woman messed up with drugs, pregnant, and about as emotionally unhinged as a person can be.

Sometimes she was clean, but the addiction always found its way back. It was in an attempt to be clean that she met my biological father – Brad Levin. Love (okay, let's keep it real, lust) was sparked and they dated. A few months later, I was in the making. Not coincidentally, that is when her relationship with Brad ended. All he was to me for most of my life was a name on my birth certificate. Everyone does what they must do at times, don't they? I can't recall ever thinking bitterly about it, not even once throughout my life.

I know when my mother passed, I wasn't angry at her or anyone. And when I finally met my biological father at age thirty-eight, I couldn't have cared any less about the past. It wasn't a priority because I'd already moved beyond the statistic I could have become and was getting along quite well in life.

Given my experiences, I learned a lot about assessing people, and this skill remains helpful to this day. I could sense when it was best to talk with my mom, avoid my mom, or just hope she didn't do anything foolish that meant someone would have to come and get her. Because if they did, that meant taking us away (again) and, although we could have been better off for it, children like to be with their parents, even if they are lousy parents.

After a few years of the single-motherhood struggle, Mom met Mark Finch and remarried. It was a lateral move at best. A bit more financial support, and it brought two more siblings – Robert and Paige.

Six mouths to feed.

A bank account usually in the single or double digits.

Cabinets and refrigerator/freezer that were often bare.

When things were bad, our grandmother (Mom's mom) would step in to fill the gaps. We were close, and we had to go stay with her on more than one occasion.

These temporary fixes were needed, but they were like putting a Band-Aid® on the Titanic. From what I observed, Mom was living in fear and uncertainty, and it showed. She had perfected verbal and physical abuse, using those as her only coping mechanism when things were tough. She was a complete authoritarian more than anything remotely resembling a mother.

During this period, a valuable lesson that's highly applicable to Servant Advisorship™ was formed – and that is the value of solid, long-term solutions for people. Temporary fixes are lazy and ineffective, guaranteed to catch up and burst open at just the wrong time.

Before long I was an older, gangly kid with acne and just about zero self-confidence, not to mention no real friends. Nothing shocking there, considering my environment. When the comparison game started, things grew agonizing in a different way.

Knowing you are poor and you can't do anything about it sucks. You can't hide it as a kid because your clothes are second-hand and your entire demeanor is one that simply begs to go unnoticed or worse, noticed.

Maybe I could have gained some skills during that time if I didn't have one other thing holding me back. I was not allowed to go anywhere or do anything. If we did go out there was a high chance, like 99.99%, that she would do something outlandish in public. That embarrassment was tough; the risk that someone who knew who I was would see it was not a risk worth taking.

Weighing good risk versus bad risk became a lifeline of sorts. You'd better do it right or you'd be dealing with the consequences of it, either at home or at school. Yes, this is also a theme that carries over into work, doesn't it? Advisors are intricately linked to the entire good-risk-versus-bad-risk concept.

Can you imagine being like my mom, acting out of fear, not love? As an adult, I get it, and it's hard for me to imagine any adult not getting it.

That said, I do remember times of love and compassion from Mom too. Rare but special. As the poet Cesare Pavese wrote, "Good thing we remember moments, not days."

Let's catch up here...

Tough lessons from Mom + strategizing survival + realizing what I did not want to have for my life = ENVISIONING MORE!

I always en*vision*ed more for my life. How could I not? It started off with adjectives like:

- Bigger
- Faster
- Better
- Stronger
- Smarter

I saw it plain as day. As a child, I remember envisioning: "Kris Bonocore in this three-piece power suit living a powerful life. I would be a CEO and run a large company. The world would be my oyster."

This was what I wanted. I knew it. But I suppressed it. Why? Good question. You see, the thought of actually doing something to make my never-endingly disappointed mother happy was something that appealed to me. So, my dream would become her dream, for a while.

Nothing changes unless you change it. (Duh.)

This was why I took massive action at age sixteen. It was up to me to change my situation. I ran away from home. Through *relentless determination*, I chose to pursue life as I envisioned it.

The night I left is vivid to me. I scaled our backyard fence and fled to a neighbor's house. They knew my situation and called some family members. Then they sent me on my way to meet up with my uncle.

Couch jumping for a period of time eventually took me from Camden County, NJ, to Montgomery County, PA.

Just being away from my old home gave me a range of new experiences that cemented I had done the right thing for me, for my life. Today, I realize the value of these life experiences and how they impact all I do. They are a valuable part of Servant Advisorship, in fact.

My Uncle Steve and his wife eventually obtained custody of me and I was able to live with them in

Lansdale, PA, until I graduated high school. This gave me time to plan my future.

It was a precise plan:

- Penn State University
- Biology major with the hopes of going to medical school to become that doctor Mom wanted me to be – a desire to please a parent is a strong one even in less-than-ideal circumstances
- Show the world what I have
- Earn money to show the world what I have

Shock alert...

College is hard work!

Study all day.

Work as a disc jockey in Philadelphia (three hours away) every weekend.

Make the vision reality.

What I didn't plan on was "fall in love."

Hellooooo Julie!

I was DJ-ing at a wedding one weekend, where I met Julie. She was a bridesmaid in the wedding. I had more confidence at this time. I was in shape. Seeing a girl didn't paralyze me. I could even talk to one without feeling like my tongue was swollen.

We began to date and shortly after in January 2000, I started an internship at Walt Disney World®. Julie and I drove to Florida together and she flew back home, then she came and visited during Spring Break – and that's when something unexpected and life-changing happened. She called me up with news: She was pregnant.

What does that statistic say about the easiest way to avoid poverty? Avoid broken homes and children out of wedlock, right?

Truth is, I don't have a redemption story. Like most people, I have a story of struggles, some blessings, and most importantly, choices.

Life's path is all about choices.

I remember the moment of my choice.

My internship ended so I immediately drove home to propose to Julie.

Thankfully, she said "yes."

I also remember the feelings I had when she said "yes." An immediate overwhelming feeling of "I need to provide," with an even stronger feeling of "I have the responsibility of keeping these two people as far away as humanly possible from the life I grew up knowing."

I wanted it to work out. However, making it all work out had grown challenging.

We were living in my in-laws' home, we had plenty of debt, I was still in school, and I was working two jobs.

I was faced with one of two choices: 1) a self-focused life, dwelling on my past struggles, or 2) a focus on the needs of others.

The results that followed have been suggested by some to be statistically impossible. Others have said it sounds like a movie script. Insiders (people who knew me) called my story the result of hard work met with a lot of good fortune.

But the truth is wrapped in one simple word: Servanthood.

I chose to focus on the needs of others.

At the moment of that choice, I was placed on the starting blocks of a new race track.

I took a job on the Philadelphia Stock Exchange as an intern, thanks to the good fortune of meeting a VP of a clearing firm who got me an in. Too much of anything is no good, except people. You can never know too many people. My network is my most valuable professional asset. More on this later.

My job at the Exchange was collecting tickets from floor traders. I immediately fell in love with the stock market and became obsessed with learning everything I could about it. So much so that I switched my school major to business/finance, which extended my graduation time quite a bit. Not much transferred from science to business. I remember calling Julie from the Exchange floor and telling her what I was doing. Needless to say, she thought I was a bit crazy.

I wanted to become a broker, so after four months on the floor of the Exchange, I sent my (meager) resume to every brokerage firm within fifty miles of where I lived (with my in-laws). I followed up each one with multiple phone calls until I received an answer. "NO" was okay with me. It was an answer. I knew that one was exhausted and to move on or keep trying (an approach that served me well in my future roles).

I finally received a call back from Scott Miller, a Senior Vice President at Morgan Stanley (back then it was called Morgan Stanley Dean Witter). We went to lunch and he agreed to hire me at $10 per hour as an unlicensed assistant. I would work from 7:30 a.m. until 1:30 p.m. most days so I could leave and make it to class by 2. I was still in college with two semesters remaining. After finishing class around 7 p.m., most nights would offer an opportunity for me to DJ at a bar and on the weekends, I would work weddings and other parties.

Long year.

I learned an incredible amount from Scott. I remember him telling me, "Don't worry about the money. Take care of your clients and your clients will take care of your money." This may very well have been the earliest professional example of Servant Advisorship™ I had witnessed.

Finally, I graduated. Now I had a degree and a year of experience. I wanted to look for another opportunity that offered upside potential. I had heard that Merrill Lynch was hiring brokers in one of their newly formed call centers. Shortly before this, Merrill Lynch had moved accounts valued at $250,000 and less away from the branch offices and to the call center, where they would be serviced and managed by brokers over the phone.

I interviewed and was hired, with the condition I pass my Series 7 and 66 exams within six months.

No problem.

I passed and began working. The call center was divided into two sites. One was just outside Princeton, NJ, and the other was in Jacksonville, FL. I worked out of the NJ location, which was about an hour from my home. Now having a wife and daughter, I wanted to be sure to be home at a reasonable time to see them. This meant arriving to work early and bringing my lunch so I could eat at my desk and conserve time.

Most of my work peers were also in their early twenties but weren't married and didn't have children. Their work time was a bit more leisurely.

Arriving early in the morning gave me an edge. Because of this, I quickly learned a great deal about the industry and the strategy of influence. (Sales is noble and necessary. I prefer to call it influence, given the connotation). Within a short period of time, I became a top-five producer between both sites and from amongst nearly 250 brokers. After only four years, I was making a six-figure income (commission-based bonuses were where the real money could be made), had been promoted to Assistant Vice President, and was leading a small team of brokers.

Massive realizations came to me during this time. We were not doing poorly or wrongly for clients, but we weren't doing the very best we could. Merrill Lynch, like many other institutions, had selling agreements with certain fund families. These limitations influenced true service. For this reason, I sought independence. I wanted to find a place where I could build something with fewer barriers to serving a client's needs better.

I discovered The Mutual Fund Store®, which offered everything I was seeking in an opportunity. The position was even to run a new office. So, I applied.

It wasn't as easy to get hired at first as I'd hoped. I'd had a long work night prior, having tried my hand in rehabbing properties to earn income.

I changed in the parking lot.

Went in and thought I interviewed great.

But where was the call?

I was persistent and kept following up. I finally connected and they said they had hired someone else. I was surprised.

Then I was even more surprised when I got a call a week or so later that the other guy wasn't going to work out after all. Did I still want the job? I did, and now I felt compelled to reveal why I felt I was a good fit for it. (Okay, some ego mixed with the start of Servant Advisorship.)

Over the course of four years, I, along with my team, grew the practice to approximately 600 households and $165 million in assets under management. This was good by any standards. I didn't do it alone and I am grateful to have developed the client relationships I did. Many of them are still dear friends today. It's one of the most rewarding feelings I know.

Next, I leapt from Advisor to Executive at one of the biggest RIA's in the country, leading hundreds of Advisors to high achievements across the country. Some of my proudest moments were guiding Advisors, perhaps like yourself, to high levels of success through Servanthood principles. This eventually led to a role leading training and employee engagement across the firm.

Today, leveraging these same principles, I lead a rapidly growing investment firm in the role of President, and I manage an intimate book of clients, because that's what I love to do.

Yes, this sounds good. I want to be unambiguous though, it was more than hard work that made all this happen. The singular defining difference in my journey began when I made the shift into Servant Advisorship.

Let's be clear. I'm not a monk or a spiritual guru. This isn't magic. What happened is a result of my choice, a choice to *serve* my wife, to *serve* my children, and to *serve* my clients as a Financial Advisor. This was my difference maker.

A choice of servanthood turned my limits into my strength.

And I'm going to teach you exactly how to do this.

While others tell you to chest thump and practice your closing skills, I'm going to share with you – and hopefully teach you at the same time – how I followed this simple Servant Advisor model.

If you do, your entire life will change like mine did.

The best part? It's simple.

You can do this. No matter what struggles you come from, no matter what stage of your career or your personal situation, I want to show you how.

I know I am damn fortunate to have been blessed with the whack alongside my head to realize this at a young age. It saved me a lot of time, and time saved upfront gives me more time to follow this bigger, bolder vision today. I will save you even more time. It will never be about me, but it is about us (Advisors) and what we can do as Servant Advisors™.

Opportunity and Tunnel Vision

Most people like to think they are making a move up when they switch jobs. This is not always the case for Advisors. Sometimes you must look around you and not just through the tunnel vision of money, because new opportunities do not mean more money all the time. With this job, I took more than a 60% pay decrease in exchange for what I was craving – an entrepreneurial, independent environment with unlimited potential.

As mentioned, my team and I grew the new office from $0 to $165 million in assets under management. My office became one of the largest and fastest-growing in company history. The exceptional part? This was also through the financial crisis, when we saw $90 million in assets under management plummet to $45 million.

How did I (really, we) do that? My small team and I worked hard, using the resources of the corporate business coupled with the Servant Advisor™ philosophy to capture market share. People wanted this new approach and we focused on making sure it was distinct and different. It was the budding of true Servant Advisorship™ as a viable business model for an entire team.

When it came to the parent company's magnificent growth, it really was a result of its franchising model. The model impressed me, and I was interested in it. As a second opportunity aside from my Advisor work, I began to raise capital so I could purchase franchise offices. In the end, I invested in offices in Pittsburgh, PA, Madison, WI, Providence, RI, and a few other places. This opportunity was insightful and positive for me, but building the client base and a team of Advisors who valued service as much as sales was where most of my focus lay.

Your people are everything, and whether you like it or not, they make your brand either work or not work. Leveraging leadership skills and inspiring others to see the value of this became my passion. It was a daily dose of invigoration, even when challenges would arise, because I saw the impact that my philosophy was having on clients. We were being remembered and recommended, we were invited into their conversations and personal decisions because we could be trusted. The support of a great parent company also helped! Servant Advisorship has this great example to inspire our growth.

The accomplishments based on a roughly sketched-out Servant Advisor model led me to the corporate opportunity for The Mutual Fund Store referenced earlier. I was eager despite the biggest adjustment, which was a move from Philadelphia to Kansas City.

What a change it all was. It was hard to gain my bearings and perspective. Like a trip to outer space, I suppose.

All that kept me focused was realizing the potential of what I could contribute. I had so much I wanted to do and so many Advisors I wished to reach.

Being responsible for a team of Advisors and other associates excited me. Not the boss part, but the part about connecting what I'd learned with other Advisors so they could do better, and maybe love what they do instead of just tolerate it as a job.

When almost five years later The Mutual Fund Store was acquired by Financial Engines®, a publicly traded company, I stayed on board and was asked to lead Training and Associate Engagement.

I was the guy to close the gaps between personnel and new expectations. Influence remained important, and learning how to use it was a must.
As an Advisor, my aspiration was to influence clients to do the right things for themselves. As a

leader, my influence shifted to the Advisors, not just face-to-face but wherever they may be in the country. How could I get them to meet the needs of clients first? (Hint: You are learning what I effectively did in those cases. They learned to operate in the spirit of a Servant Advisor and now have that same opportunity.)

Yes, I was busy.

The Role of Relentless Determination

You are focused each day on what you feel it takes to succeed at what you need to do.

I call this "relentless determination." This phrase means everything to me and it has always played a major role in my life. Without it, today would not be what it is for me.

And how much do I mean that phrase when thought or voiced? Enough that I have not hesitated a single time to pursue actions that are fueled by it.

On the surface, it appears that being relentlessly determined is kind of easy. No skill, training, or education needed – just a desire. You won't find any test or acronym on your business card to show you have it. Therefore, it appears fluffy and meaningless. I disagree! I am relentlessly determined. I'm the guy you want in your foxhole.

Initially, the word "relentless" projects a negative connotation. "This salesman is *relentless*, he won't stop calling me!" Change the context and change the perspective. "His relentless optimism helped keep the team unified." Or, "His unrelenting praise was inspiring."

By viewing "relentless" in this manner, the power in the word lies in which direction it travels.

"Relentless" is usually negatively viewed when one is the object of it. Nobody welcomes it in this context, including me. "The predator was relentless in pursuit of his prey." I picture someone hiding in a corner, flat-out avoiding anything relentless.

However...

Deliver relentlessness and you deliver energy and focus toward a target you want to:

- Attract
- Acquire
- Attain

Furthermore, when relentlessness is applied to pursuing something inanimate such as a dream, a goal, or a vision, it becomes a super-power word.

For example, water is relentless as it flows through a canyon, never deterred by any rock or other obstacle in its way (I've always idolized Bruce Lee).

There is power in being relentless. Think of:

- Will and Skill
- Science and Art
- Effort and Effectiveness
- Energy and Focus

These words pairings are important to the work of a Servant Advisor™. Each describes what a Servant Advisor needs in order to be initially successful and continually grow his/her practice.

- Will, Science, Effort, and Energy describes activities an Advisor does daily.
- Skill, Art, Effectiveness, and Focus describes how activities are done.

A symbiotic relationship exists. These words cannot operate independently of each other for Servant Advisors. Desired results aren't achieved by compromising the strength of the process.

Now I'm going to throw out a word that is overused and usually under-delivered upon. Ready? FOCUS.

We must focus on our vision. Think about it, write about it, talk about it. There's no other way to make it clearer to us and the world around us.

Focus on the right areas. Paying too much attention to obstacles and challenges is hindering. It's a bummer, hardly inspirational. Focus, like anything else, can be either productive or destructive.

Newton's Law of Inertia states objects in motion stay in motion with the same speed and in the same direction. Unless… acted upon by an unbalanced force. Relentless determination is like inertia.

I've been "acted upon" more times than I enjoy admitting. Some were self-induced and other things that were meant to come my way.

For example, in my work at Merrill Lynch, I had 10 to 12-hour days for nearly five years. I wanted to learn all I could, be a top performer, and earn an income that would meet my family's needs – and wants. Despite my growth, I also experienced downsides, such as the long commute and constraints on: 1) what I could say; 2) what I could do; 3) who I could talk to; and 4) my growth was limited to phone work only.

Good opportunity.

Still, a limited opportunity.

I longed for growth and was living in the shadows of a confined environment.

**There are many Advisors like me –
those who want to grow independently
and entrepreneurially.**

If you desire to build something, you know that starting over every quarter is not a long-term plan to success.

I wanted to move from "How can I sell you?" to "How can I help you?" I also wanted to meet clients and build trusting relationships. Knowing I gave them my best unhindered advice and wisdom meant something to me. As an Advisor, does that sound great to you? How about as a client? Would you love to know you're being treated superbly – and from the heart – by a professional you rely on, whether it's a CPA, lawyer, insurance agent, and so on?

All of this leads me back to the opportunity I found in The Mutual Fund Store.

They were leaders I wanted to follow. I knew the company's founder Adam Bold meant what he said and had conviction. Never doubted it.

These resources and culture gave me an amazing canvas to do two things:

1. Work toward my personal vision
2. Help the population of prospective clients who were attracted to our model

NEWS ALERT: We can do what's best for us as individuals and what's best for our client at the same time. It is not an "either/or" choice.

Now, let's talk about determination.

Everyone is or has been determined to do something.

I've been determined to get good grades, win a race, be a good father and husband, and work out once a day. I've even been determined to get a good night's rest once or twice.

The word "determination" describes persistence, grit, willingness, and resilience. It's a desire to do something.

Determination is meaningful to me and I consider it a part of my DNA and prefer the same from others. I look for this when interviewing someone. It gives me an indication of whether they will succeed. It trumps other skills, unless it is a specialty position.

What challenges have you had? How did you overcome them? These and other questions reveal compelling components of human nature. Your story may not be so raw and crazy like mine, but it is your story that has sculpted you in some way. The downtrodden and uber wealthy both make mistakes, mischaracterize situations, and need to learn life lessons. No one is special in that way, thankfully.

Give me someone who has been knocked down and gotten back up, and I'll show you a winner.

Make mistakes.

Learn from them.

Keep moving onward.

View failure as an opportunity to begin again with a bit more wisdom and experience. It is an educational gift. Maybe a costly one, but a gift nonetheless.

Skill can easily be taught; will is far more difficult to teach or elicit. Talent is good, but perseverance is far more desirable.

"Ordinary adults have a strong ability to change with practice, but if you have a fixed mind set, you don't think you can improve your intelligence, you will probably not improve. The region of the brain responsible for controlling fingers in young musicians grew in direct proportion to the number of years training. Purposeful practice builds new neural connections in your brain, so you can improve aspects of your 'intelligence' with practice." – From the book "Bounce" by Michael Syed

I've always been determined to provide superior customer service, whether as a disc jockey, a waiter, or an Advisor. To me, client experience and service to the client has been and will always be paramount. At first, sure, it was my money maker. Waiters don't make much if they are jerks or unresponsive. But with time and maturity, my vision grew. This growth can take place in all of us. Has yours grown? If it hasn't, you're lurking in the poisonous waters of stagnation.

Don't confuse all this with perfection, though. Even someone committed to integrity faces big challenges. One of my biggest challenges happened after I was "free sailing and separated" from my childhood chaos.

In May 2017, I learned my wife of seventeen years, the love of my life, had fallen out of love with me. I could not believe it. I'd strived for perfection for her and my family – at least that's what I believed.

Forced reflections were both excruciating and enlightening.

My determination had failed me in a monumental way.

Even though I'd built a career, a company, and a lifestyle with determination, I neglected part of my "why" for doing that.

Julie had been taken for granted for so long. I never disrespected her. She had complete freedom to do what she wanted all the time. I thought this was right. I thought that I was supposed to go to work and make money so she could enjoy her life without any worry.

I thought…wrong!

I had not applied the same principles of Servant Advisorship™ to my marriage. My focus had been absent – even if I had a hard time seeing it right away. My pursuit of success had failed a major part of my inspiration, my wife.

When I found this out, we made more choices, all with Julie's complete support. I would walk away from my career, we would leave Kansas City, and we would start anew in Florida. It was more critical that we rebuilt our foundation and save our family than it was for me to continue my career path.

Easy choice.

We made these big choices quickly and had no second doubts about it. I was all in to fix what meant so much. Any vision of my life included more than me, it also included Julie and our children. They are irreplaceable, and money is not. A career is not. A job is not. Family is.

Everything we did was worth it.

In Florida, my focus was entirely on our family. I dedicated myself to trying to rebuild what had begun to deteriorate. The scariest nightmare I could have was to think of a life without all of us together. This massive-action decision is one of the smartest choices I've ever made. It taught me so much and reminded me of how to be a true servant, which means I am a servant in all areas of my life, not just professionally.

To be a servant, there is no picking or choosing. We are all in or we are not in at all.

I recognize my blessings for my opportunity to do what I did. Have you ever been in a similar situation? You were working so hard at what you thought everyone else needed that you lost sight of the message. I thought I was more aware, but I'd been in a tunnel that I didn't even realize I'd entered.

And Julie...she saw my relentless determination firsthand.

Determination is about intentionality, producing the desired outcome.

**Train your mind to desire
what the situation demands.**

When you have a purpose, great things happen. Suddenly you are meaningful in your thoughts and actions, giving them the energy and focus necessary to achieve the desired outcome. These experiences have meaning and their significance sticks with us.

One of the best books I've found to cover this topic is *Relentless: From Good to Great to Unstoppable* by Tim S. Grover. In this book, Grover shares thirteen things extremely successful people do. He describes their mindset, work ethic, and how these areas make them unstoppable. The concepts in the book are raw and may give you pause, not unlike the word "relentless," as discussed earlier. They're also about commitment, a commitment to success with fewer obstacles and setbacks.

If we do not control our own journey, who will? We must dictate what we need to do or someone else will be glad to tell us what to do.

From an early age, I was relentlessly determined on both a large scale and a small scale.

As a young child, I remember practicing magic repeatedly. It wasn't a fad, but an obsession. I would practice, show others my tricks, and practice some more. I also remember learning how to do things such as headstands, flip quarters off my elbow, brainteasers, physical challenges, play pool, and juggle. I worked to perfect each one. It's all I did at times, until I mastered it. Over and over and over again.

What was interesting about all these pursuits was my mother's response. She'd tell me to "stop being obsessed." For me, it was about the results. I was obsessed with the outcomes, including the effects they had on people.

In my late teens and early twenties, fitness became my obsession. I would go to the gym for hours at a time. I read about training, wrote out training programs, and trained others as well as myself. Once again, I loved the results and how I could impact others with nutrition and training.

As I grew into adulthood, I became relentlessly determined in my professional life. Work consumed me. At first, I knew I had to learn, so in my role at Morgan Stanley, I listened, watched, read, wrote, asked questions, made mistakes, and arrived early, all in an effort to build a foundation. It was all about learning. Energy and focus. There was no other path to advance to the next level in the industry. Money had nothing to do with it, which is why even then I knew to be comfortable with $10 per hour.

All this commitment was part of a bigger vision. Goals are milestones on the path toward a vision.

When I chose to leave home at sixteen, the road was not easy, but I made a choice to maintain the path toward my vision. I had little confidence in myself. I lived with my uncle but was basically alone, trying to finish high school with 3,000 other kids while staying clear of drugs and building up my confidence. My vision was strong, so my confidence continued to improve as I progressed forward, enduring life's natural, unexpected jabs and punches.

A winner gets up every time he or she is knocked down. I've been knocked down plenty of times, but I always refused to stay down.

"It's impossible to beat a person who refuses to give up." – Babe Ruth

Our vision is our ideal outcome. In order for our ideal outcome to be realized, it is essential to first define what, in fact, success is.

What does success mean to you? Think on this for a minute.

Only you can define what your success is. It's different for each Advisor, as each has a different set of goals or vision he or she has identified.

What is your starting point? And how can I help get you there?

It's difficult to hit a target you cannot see.

If you want to have precision, you need to know your "why."

- Why do you want to go to work each morning?
- Why does what you're doing serve your purpose?
- Why do you want to assign a goal to or determine a vision for yourself?

When we have something to work toward, we don't meander.

When we're directionless, we're working toward nothing.

Define a personal, meaningful vision that you will be motivated to pursue each day, and it will give you purpose. Without this, the pages and rhetoric ahead will be of little use.

Not sure about the entire concept of a vision? You'll enjoy that chapter tremendously, and by its end, you'll know what a vision is and how to bring yours to fruition.

Real magic only happens outside your comfort zone.

Unlike many people, I do not believe that luck simply happens. Most walk into a casino playing to win and hoping for luck, as if it's some unearthly force that descends upon us.

Too often I hear, "he's so lucky," or "she always wins." There is no way this is true! There are strategies for improving your odds of success at a casino, as in most other aspects of life – but hope is not a strategy. It leaves everything to chance.

However, I do believe luck is created. Be intentional and take steps in situations to help you increase the probability of success. This is creating luck.

My son Ethan has a sign on his bathroom wall that reads: *Never Give Up. Go Over, Go Under, Go Around, or Go Through, but Never Give Up.* He chose to put it up when we moved into our home.

Interestingly, my daughter Madison was the one who bought the sign during a family vacation. It's a pleasure to see the values and qualities of relentless determination appear in my children. For me, it's the beginning of a legacy.

**No fear, no limits. The only limits we have
are the ones we place on ourselves.**

It is not easy to think this way. It takes time to build up this kind of resilience and confidence. And confidence is crucial for relentless determination. We must have the confidence in our vision and in ourselves. We must believe the vision is achievable and that we have the resources to work toward it.

I'm a baseball enthusiast. As a child, I loved baseball and as a parent, I was fortunate enough to be able to coach both my children (softball was close enough).

Hitting a baseball requires confidence above all else. Without confidence in your skills and ability to connect, you are likely to miss. It makes sense how this same concept would hold true in life, doesn't it? Without confidence, you cannot work toward a vision. And this is important because... relentless determination is strongest when our vision is clearest.

I am going to offer you a bit of relief. Vision creation is a skill that can be developed. So is relentless determination, which is an extension of this. Understand, the direct proportion of how clear a vision is reveals itself in our results. I've relied on understanding this almost my entire life, even before I truly understood what I was doing. I am thankful for my inherent instincts, however.

What's Your Story?

Redefine your story. If not today, when?

I find it inspirational to act right away. Waiting is the same as procrastinating in these situations.

It all doesn't have to be perfect to begin.

There is no more ideal time than now.

Organizing is endless if we allow it to be.

Planning is great, but no plan remains the same once acted upon.

Just commit to doing something (or things) differently in your life so you can improve your results.

Maybe it's finding the positives in life's tough lessons from the past.

Perhaps it is being honest with yourself about what your effort-to-results ratio has been thus far.

Knowing your story could even be defining what is missing in your life and your career as an Advisor.

Don't be afraid to ask yourself the tough questions and dive in, not only in your personal life, but also with your career.

Questions worth considering:

- **Do I serve my clients' best interests or my own?** For Advisors, impossibility is defined as believing you can do the best for clients when you are more focused on your paycheck, your results, your accolades.

- **Do I sell clients or serve clients?** Selling products and services doesn't serve peoples' best interests. Could the product you sell be the best one for them? Absolutely. But if you ponder, "Would I sell them this product even if it wasn't the best one for them?" and you hesitate or cannot say "no," then you are practicing selling over serving.

- **Would I like to become the trusted Advisor my clients rely on for more than just investment advice?** If you thought "no," perhaps it is time to find a new career. However, if you thought "yes," you are expressing a healthy desire to work within the parameters of what a Servant Advisor™ is – a trusted source for insights in other areas of a client's life.

Embrace life's lessons that have brought you to today. Realize you can "teach an old dog new tricks." Start shifting your perspective to that of a Servant Advisor.

Servant Advisors possess qualities that guide strong relationships. It's a philosophy to goodness that reminds us all that *it's not about me.*

Part Two | Walking the Walk

"Earn your success based on service to others, not at the expense of others."

- H. Jackson Brown, Jr.

Are you ready to adopt the Servant Advisor™ concept? I don't mean dwell on it, toss it around, or put it on the back burner for another day. Adopt it now. Your clients are ready. The industry is in need.

We need a belief system and philosophy – a guiding set of principles – to anchor us Advisors in our commitment. It is the easiest way to adhere to what's required of us individually (no one else) and stay on course as best we can during those busy days and exhausted nights.

Ensuring we are focused on giving our clients what they need can be a whole lot different than focusing on what clients may claim they want.

My evolution took time. I would have gone at the speed of light if I could have, but it was more of a "hero's journey." Recognize a challenge, realize you're the solution, and then prove you've got what it takes. That kind of thing.

The process I've used compounds all the experiences I've had in my career. Being diligent about the learning I was committed to was essential, and with no shortcuts or easy pathways. For any of us to do this, we need Herculean strength at times, which is why we must continually:

- Evolve
- Grow
- Learn

**Servant Advisors don't just arrive;
we are a continual work in progress.**

I know that by calling myself a Servant Advisor today, I am not guaranteed to remain a Servant Advisor tomorrow, or even to be better. That's a fact.

This evolution has challenges that want to knock us down, especially those Advisors who still work in investment firms where they do not subscribe to clients' best interests over their own bottom line.

This isn't about putting other firms down; this is all about lifting Advisors up. For those of us who want to be the best, we understand the necessity to have best practices. Pretty simple, really.

So why make it complicated?

We can all choose not to go against our values and to approach our work with the right mindset. It works in the office, at home, and in our community when we do this.

I believe in free-flowing options. One solution doesn't fit all.

We need to have a certain level of freedom to dive into the right choices for clients, and that is what I will offer those who choose to take this exciting, and not entirely easy, journey.

No entrepreneur was built in a day!

And let's not kid ourselves; it's an entrepreneurial mindset that gives us the grit to bear all we have gone through and have yet to go through. It's not as bad as emergency surgery, but a time or two it might feel like a Band-Aid is slowly being peeled off of a sunburn. Don't be startled by the thought; be inspired to be tougher than whatever comes your way. It works!

To counter this and exemplify what a Servant Advisor does:

- Continually improving products, services, and offerings;
- Making sure we're doing our part in creating a constructive environment for other Advisors;
- Showing other Advisors how to start practicing the principles of a Servant Advisor; and,
- Seeking out new knowledge and concepts to remain fresh and relevant. In turn, we are (and we can all become) better Advisors for our clients.

How do you think you rate as an Advisor if you currently are one? If you're not sure, consider this: Would you ever ask a group of people (who didn't know you were an Advisor) what they thought about Financial Advisors, in general? It might be hard to take the heat from that question – the heat being that which is creeping up your neck in the discomfort of their thoughts of you.

You've got to get the big picture…

No matter where we Advisors work from, clients will always expect service and to be well taken care of. This can be faked for a bit, given a personality or a firm's expectations, but the ruse cannot go on for long. After a bit, clients realize, *hey, they're not in this for me, they're in this for them*. This thought doesn't stem from bad Advisors as much as it does from being trapped in a system that no longer works for today's needs.

I've got the tools and resources for you right now. It's up to you to run wild with them and create the system of service needed to get a glimpse into what incredible customer service and client/Advisor relationships look and feel like.

Committed Servant Advisors seldom-to-never experience the lashing out and disdain other Advisors are susceptible to. Clients are assured of:

- Their needs being understood
- Their Servant Advisor knowing how to find the best approach for their needs
- An ability to trust their Advisor with other big questions in life
- Being a priority

Look, even Servant Advisors are clients to someone. We all love to know we are being sincerely and adequately taken care of. If we weren't, we would not be content to stay with mediocre. This is true because certain aspects of human nature are the same, one being that sticking with professionals who don't meet a need when choices are available isn't a "have to."

I left Merrill Lynch for a reason. We weren't doing badly for clients, but we were restricted in terms of the products we could use – only the mutual funds that the firm had a relationship with and they had to be within an allocation model we were "allowed" to use.

A massive variety of products were available within the investing universe, just not to us.

Because clients' needs are limitless, I prefer limitless options, and I believe all of us do.

Serving clients from the heart and with a mindset of their needs being met is rewarding. It's the only way. Let me say that again: It's the only way.

If you feel the power of this, you are someone who believes in the philosophy of being a Servant Advisor.

Servant Advisors are pioneers on the new frontier of expectations for financial services. There is a huge demand for them and a lack of supply.

We are now connected because we both sense this but need a resource in order to make it happen.

Imagine…

We're all gathered in a conference room and the energy is rising. Relentless determination is surfacing and compelling everyone forward. We are amid a group of like-minded Advisors realizing a better way to serve the client. This community keeps growing and growing…

In time, all people have the option of accessing a Servant Advisor's help. It doesn't matter if they are skeptical, cautious, new to investments, or know exactly what they want – they all have a place at the table of a Servant Advisor, because there is one goal: Serving the client's needs remarkably well.

This is my vision.

Part Three | Seeing is Believing

"If you hire people just because they can do a job, they'll work for your money. But if you hire people who believe what you believe, they'll work for you with blood and sweat and tears."

\- Simon Sinek

I am a visual person. Everything is easier for me when I can use a visual approach to understand it. This is true of everything from landmarks to layouts to private information. As a child, I used to ask people for information like credit card and Social Security numbers just to show I could memorize them. Obviously, that was a different world than what we caution people about today.

Opposite to vision is being blind. Not literally, but blind by choosing not to be in the light. Take the archer; how can he or she hit a target if they are blindfolded or there is no light? It becomes a nearly impossible task.

A clear vision about my life and my expectations within it has always existed. I knew what I wanted and could place a vision to the desire.

I saw the type of car I wanted to drive, the house I wanted to live in, and even the mannerisms I wanted to display. Most importantly, I knew the overwhelming feeling I wanted to experience in my life when I reached these milestones. Mine would be a life filled with:

- Confidence
- Security
- Freedom
- Independence

Visions are our deals.

However...

It's a rare reality to become precisely what we envision.

This doesn't mean we stop trying to understand and know precisely what we are working toward. It sounds complicated and tough; missing the mark is something none of us desire to do. We want to touch what we can achieve.

Have you heard of an asymptote? It's a geometrical term referring to lines getting as close to each other as theoretically possible without touching.

Here's an illustration:

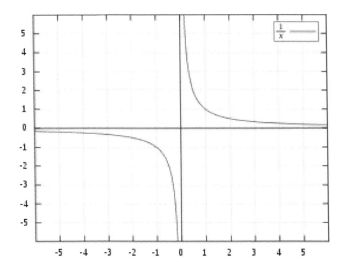

You still with me? Trust me, this does lead to vision.

Taking all this into account, understanding of the idea of an asymptote requires an effort of reason rather than experience, as do visions.

Visions require reason and belief. We have never experienced our precise vision, but we must believe it is within reach.

75

Okay, Kris, great, but isn't that really a goal?

No, it's not. You see, goals are milestones toward a vision.

Simon Sinek, the popular author and speaker well known for *Start with Why*, separates vision and goals this way:

A goal has a defined finish line. You can track the metrics and know when you've completed the goal. A vision is having a crystal-clear idea of what the finish line looks like, but you have no idea how far away it is. You may never achieve the level you envision, but the drive, passion and joy to reach it is constant.

As for dreams, they are merely a vision without action. Nice, but not as effective.

The process of a vision is what most people seek and value. It's never the finished product because that doesn't exist. It can't be when we commit to continually evolve.

Take the time to view your achievements in this manner. It's quite powerful. We can begin realizing we could and would do a job we love for free and derive great satisfaction from it. Would the money follow? Most likely, but it's not the driving motivator.

Being driven by money is very low on most successful people's list of what's important. Not just because they have money, but because they know it's not powerful in their vision.

Many people stop when they reach their FIRST barrier when in pursuit of a goal. It's sad to invest effort in an idea to never even see the prize behind the wall. People with winning attitudes and actions will never settle for an easy fail. Take a long look at what you've settled for and what you need to change.

Vision and Value

To formulate a clear vision, we must first understand what is valued.

True vision has nothing to do with our product or solution. It reflects:

- Who we are
- Who we are driven to become

Our vision is an insight into our core values and beliefs. It evokes emotion and is futuristic, as we are always moving toward it.

There is also power in a vision. It can unite people in:

- Business
- Their community
- A cause

In business, we need to thoughtfully construct visions that get at the root of what brought the founders to the table in the first place. For a similar reason, it is what brings customers to the table too.

This is so important.

Customers want to be part of the movement. They want to participate in something they believe in. At The Mutual Fund Store, we believed in our founder Adam Bold's vision. He believed investors owed it to themselves to be in the best funds possible. As Advisors, we chose funds for our clients because they had the best fund managers possible, not because of the names on the funds. We had no attachment to any one fund, because this approach demonstrated we were serving our clients' best interests. Consequently, this is what helped to grow The Mutual Fund Store at a rapid rate. Clients knew what we were about and wanted to be a part of it.

What do you or your firm stand for? What do you believe in?

A great example of a vision with a belief is attached to the great Dr. Martin Luther King, Jr. People bought into his belief and still follow it to this day. It's so powerful! It's now fifty-plus years later and people still know and understand his vision. They talk about it and teach it.

Supporting efforts that deeply resonate with time, energy, values, and freedoms feels instinctually right. We wear our belief on our clothes, put stickers on our cars, and tell our friends about it.

What is amazing about a good vision is that when we tell our friends, it seldom has anything to do with what a business makes or offers. That doesn't matter as much as feeling connected to them on a deeper level.

Case Study: New Belgium Brewery

If you like artisan beer, you've likely heard of New Belgium Brewery. They are a microbrewery with a handful of beers on the national market. Fat Tire is one of their more successful brews.

But is Fat Tire what makes New Belgium Brewery a great company to talk about? Not really. New Belgium is fun to talk about because of their support and belief in their people and our planet.

Many people know these things about New Belgium Brewery, all which are reflective of their vision:

- Their employees came together and decided to forgo bonuses for five years so the company could afford to convert to green energy.
- The brewery gives all employees the famous red bike after one year of service.
- After five years of service, employees receive a paid trip to Belgium.

You can't get much more fun and unique benefits than that!

How do these benefits influence us, the consumer? We want to be a part of the New Belgium values so much that we align with them. People align with New Belgium by drinking their beer and telling their friends about the cool things they do.

You've hit the mark when people are willing to gather socially and talk about a company culture more than the product!

Have you ever worked at a company like that? Not many have.

New Belgium has also listed Ten Core Values on their website. Among them are:

- "Kindling social, environmental and cultural change as a business role model"
- "Environmental stewardship – honoring nature at every turn of the business"
- "Cultivating potential through learning, high involvement culture, and the pursuit of opportunities"
- "Trusting each other and committing to authentic relationships and communications"
- "Having fun"

I'd bet one or more of the values listed above have you feeling, *I want that. I want to aspire to carrying out those values, and I'd love to be a part of a family, group, or business that shares values like those.* This is an example where values meet the vision.

Values like New Belgium's awake, motivate, and inspire their employees and make people want to become one of those employees too.

Reflect on a tough situation in your current work environment. Then think of New Belgium's values. I bet you see some guidance as to how you should behave or respond in any tough situation. Values remind us of better choices. They provide something for us to anchor to.

Servant Advisors™ have a tremendous opportunity to create a vision like this for their clients.

We can grow an advisory practice with employees who are aligned with the Servant Advisor lifestyle. Make no mistake about it, it's a lifestyle. One cannot be someone else outside of work and believe they are a Servant Advisor behind their desk. Any other viewpoint is a lie.

Are you only married in front of your spouse? Are you only a parent when your kids are present? Of course not. Be reasonable and don't kid yourself about this type of topic.

The Psychology of Visions

We talked about the difference between a vision and a goal earlier (reminder: goals are milestones on the way to achieving a vision). Understanding this isn't enough. Knowing how to apply it all so it works is required.

Big questions for you...

- What is your vision?
- How do you create it?

To lay out a highly impactful and culture-creating vision, you must know who you are first. Be attuned to what makes you tick. Start with the negatives:

- What personal boundaries do I have?
- What instantly and personally sets me off?
- What actions by others do I view as disrespectful?

Now, let's move to the positives:

- What gets me excited and inspires me?
- What changes am I driven to stand for?
- What value do I bring to the table?

Now, these answers aren't cut and dry. They can sting like sweat in your eye or daze you like you were just on a day-long Tilt-A-Whirl™ ride.

If you need to go deeper, do it!

For example, contemplate why you get upset when co-workers or excuse-makers don't take ownership of their mistakes. It could be because you value honor, accountability, honesty, learning, or curiosity.

Go through both these categories to identify what you value. Our values are wonderful ways to act in a Servant Advisor™ capacity that helps us to connect with our clients – they'll understand what we value, and many times it can be the same things they value too.

Our values are ever-present, even if they're subconscious and even if we refuse to pay attention to what they are. When our values are not clear, how to act, react, or behave in a given situation is unclear and our confidence to execute is low.

When we admit what's important to us and our values become crystal clear, who we are designed to be surfaces. Our confidence to act becomes solid, unwavering.

I have often found myself considering worst case scenarios such as, would I treat this person differently today if I knew they were going to die tomorrow? Perhaps it's because of the negative experiences I've had but, yes, I do this. This is called negative visualization.

Negative visualization sounds like something we'd all like to avoid, doesn't it? Conversely, it is exactly what many people use to create a powerful and compelling vision that they know, with absolute certainty, is something they want.

The premise of the negative visualization is to contemplate outcomes in your life by seeing what you have and visualizing your life without them.

For example, if you have a spouse you love tremendously, think about what life would be like without him or her. I experienced this firsthand when I was so involved with pursuits of being a Servant Advisor that I tossed those principles out the window when it came time to be a Servant Husband. This is a very effective example of negative visualization.

The other type of visualization is the one most people are familiar with – positive visualization, where you see the life you want minus situations not favorable to it.

No matter how you pursue your vision or what form of it you feel would be most effective for you, there are two phases to its creation:

1. Create your vision in your head.
2. Work toward your vision again in real life.

Now, it may not be as simplistic as a 1-2 punch, but there are no other options. You create and duplicate, or you go back to the drawing board. This happens all the time.

Maybe it was a wrong vision and you weren't inspired to act, or you need to tweak it to become a bit wiser.

How many times have we all been there?

Did you notice anything else about the two phases for vision?

Review them one more time.

Maybe you'll notice the first one (create the vision in your head) is mental and the second (work toward your vision in real life) is physical. It's the combination of both that helps it all to happen.

Many people recognize this as the Law of Attraction, or Law of Manifestation. It takes the right thoughts to cast our desires out into the universe, combined with the proper actions to show we want it – not kind of want it or are interested in it, but the I HAVE TO HAVE IT type of want it.

There are numerous metaphors for it. Don't talk the talk if you can't walk the walk…and so on.

Simon Sinek says that to attract the attention of clients and create a long-lasting business, the business must know why they do what they do. This is central to his Golden Circle – a Ted Talk and 12-minute video he did that's worth watching. He talks about the idea that people don't buy what you do, they buy why you do it. One powerful point of the video shares how you cannot ask your customers why they do business with you. Why? Because they cannot tell you!

People seldom know the specifics of why they do business with someone. This is because the part of the brain that controls behavior does not control language. So essentially, customers rationalize price, service, quality, and features.

Introducing the next logical question: If customers cannot explain why they do what they do or why they use a specific company product or service, how can any individual or business led by individuals explain why they do what they do? Contrary to some opinions, I believe they can. You just must be willing to do the work.

Think about it...most people cannot even tell you their goals. Try asking once; ask someone what they are saving for. They may say retirement. Okay, fair, but what does that look like? What do you want to do in retirement? What does retirement feel like and look like? What is the vision for retirement? How much will that cost? How does a person know they on track to retire with what they'll to cover costs associated with retirement?

Or try another question: How did you choose to be a [fill in the profession]? What are your career goals? Some may answer this fine, but most, like Simon says, will rationalize. I like it, it feels good, I get to help people. But what does any of that even mean?

Revealing and articulating why we do what we do and the goals we have is achievable. People just need help understanding how to do it – how to dig to that level of depth, and how to be in tune with who they are and why they behave the way they do.

Knowing your "why" is not easy. Fortunately!

It's a task worth pursuing and it's rewarding in its revelations, both as an Advisor and in our lives, in general.

Sure, we can surround the "why" with power words and phrases that sound nice and make us feel good. But...I bet doing that leaves most feeling flat, unmotivated, and unable to drive past the feelings of fear, risk adversity, and low confidence.

How do we overcome this? A smart approach is to make a vision clear enough that fears become irrelevant.

See what could become, not what's keeping you from it.

Develop this skill. It takes work and strong mental muscles to maintain it.

When it's present, there is no room for fear.

The fears my mother instilled in me began to dissipate when I began working toward my vision.

More so, a vision is not limited; there are no rules or restrictions. It engages our senses beyond just sight.

We feel it and hear it; we know just how it would play out.

It is the future, a time travel mechanism. We become what we envision our self to be. It makes no room for dour visions of being a failure or never getting the new opportunity.

I believe people predominantly reside in one of three timeframes: past, present, or future.

Thinking out into the future works for me. I was walking with a friend recently who asked why I was always thinking five years ahead. I said, "I'm going to spend all of my time in the future so why not work on building it the way I want it. It's also the one I can have the most influence on."

Yes, it's true. The past is gone, the present is here already, and tomorrow is not yet determined. Why not think about the future and create it the way you want it?

Of course, we'll meet present thinkers and past dwellers in your life. There is no right or wrong to thinking this way. All ways of thinking have pros and cons, which is why we need to evaluate what serves us best personally and professionally.

All that said, I've shared my past, and I am going to ask you to indulge me in the topic of "the past" for a bit longer. If I'd clung to my past, as rocky as parts of it were, my journey would be very different.

The past also serves as a source of reminders so we don't forget to participate in our outcome. This is logical. Still, the past can be a big obstacle. It can hinder us from achieving the life we want and can alter our thinking because we're fearful of repeating old mistakes.

Lisa Firestone Ph.D., clinical psychologist, author, and the Director of Research and Education for the Glendon Association, said: *"Once you recognize the undesirable ways your past is affecting your present behavior, you can make a conscious effort to act differently. You can teach yourself to stop reacting instinctively and to really think about the kind of person you want to be."*

Reacting instinctively off the past makes us reactionary about the future – but not necessarily with the best information. Think of this in a Servant Advisor capacity. No one's best interests are served when we look to the future without the best insights and information.

No wonder why this is so challenging! The solution exists by our knowing our hurdles. This is how we reduce limitations associated with vision creation. There are three elements to understanding this.

1. **From early childhood on, we've been conditioned to make life decisions based on limited information.**

   It is easy to make a choice based on what is in front of us. It is what's most readily available.

   Creating a vision demands us to draw from an infinite range of choices. It is uncomfortable to do this. Thankfully! Comfort zones are dangerous places. Growth and expansion do not exist within these zones.

   "Ever since I was a child, I have had this instinctive urge for expansion and growth. To me, the function and duty of a quality human being is the sincere and honest development of one's potential." – Bruce Lee

2. **Visualization is a skill.**

   Aside from being a skill, visualization operates like a muscle. Most people stop using this muscle in childhood.

We forget how to visualize, we forget how to dream. We forget there are no true limitations in life, and that the only limitations are the ones we create with our minds.

It feels uncomfortable or too challenging to visualize our future. Many people tell themselves they can't, or it doesn't work for them. This is an excuse, a complete falsity. The more we visualize, the better we become at creating from our imagination.

Don't tell me you're shocked to hear you'll get better with practice. Most of us have heard this our entire lives, but we've chosen to ignore it. Maybe we don't like the source it's coming from or we simply are too defiant to let the words absorb.

Absorb them today if this sounds like you.

3. **We're afraid of our vision.**

The unlimited range of options we must draw upon for a vision can be scary, especially if it involves our success. We question our competence, our ability to persevere. We are uncertain of our value:

- Am I worthy of thinking big?
- Do I have the resources to think big and visualize an ideal future?

So many people answer "no" to these questions. They go into what they do not have. Maybe they feel they're lacking a pedigree, genetics, a good upbringing, whatever. These are not valid reasons to play it small in life. Safety cannot always win out over growth.

Reflect on you, the Advisor. Do you think small? If you do, you are doing yourself a great disservice. Find the strength tied to a bigger vision – a Servant Advisor-driven vision.

Now evaluate how your actions measure up to your values. Are you living out what you say you stand for? This can be tough, especially when the weights of the real world are always in play. I'm referring to relationships, finances, children, and so on.

Manifestation's Role in Vision

Some people have suggested you should cling tightly to your visions, but I pose the contrary to you.

Share your visions with others.

Be fearless about this and, even if it's out of the realm of all conceivable possibilities, don't be dissuaded.

Even if you don't have a clear path yet, don't be deterred.

Share proudly.

Share openly.

Be bold.

All of this is manifestation – defined as an event or action which embodies something you have theorized, or also an abstract idea. Incredible, powerful stuff.

Imagine what we could accomplish if we put these great thoughts about doing excellent things toward helping others. I've done it and I want to help you do the same. If people knew they could go talk to an Advisor who always had their best interests at heart – they just knew it – that is powerful. I am that Advisor.

**Speak confidently in terms of
what you *will* do, not what you *could*
do or *would* do but what *will* be.**

We now know that a vision is both mental and physical. In addition, it is a tool we can use to take us through many situations so we can move past them and continue forward on our pursuits. How can a vision be used? Here are a few ways:

- To define the way we conduct our business
- To keep our purpose clear
- To overcome obstacles
- To maintain focus
- To stay inspired

With manifestation, we can take a strong and current vision and connect it with our passions and greatest potential. Then, incredible things begin to happen.

Suddenly, neither whatever is going wrong in the world nor the challenges that present themselves cripple us. We manage them – they are like that obstacle mentioned earlier. We acknowledge, solve, and navigate through them and continue on with bringing our vision closer. It's hard not to embrace the concept of living our life this way. It's amazing.

When we pave our life's path with a vision, we feel more valuable as a person when we set and achieve the goals toward it.

A leader's vision gains them the ability to see today as it is and calculate a future that grows and improves. A successful leader can see the future and still stay focused on the present. It's no coincidence the most poignant leaders of our time, people like Steve Jobs, Richard Branson, Martin Luther King, Jr., and Winston Churchill, understood the importance of creating visions and then executing on them.

These pioneers spent endless hours bringing their visions into reality. What's incredible about witnessing this (or the result of it) is the lack of evidence indicating they got tired along the way. I'm sure they did. I get tired some days, but feeling tired does not stop me from manifesting the vision.

How close have you come to this place in your life, in your career? It's infectious and kind of like centrifugal force – once it starts, it does not stop.

Visions are strong forces for everyone who has one. In business, they become the target upon which a leader focuses resources and energy. This type of vision will do many things.

- The continual presence of a vision helps to motivate against forces of resistance: failure, emotional hardships (negative feedback), and real hardships (issues in the company).
- When a vision spreads through a company, it pushes both the leaders and employees toward the same goals together rather than separately. Visions can successfully turn a corporate hierarchy into a harmonious and well-organized group.
- A leader's vision can be embraced by others with proper communication. It can be discussed and perfected by all of those who are vested in it and believe it.
- When a vision is powerful, it becomes the glue that holds together individuals of a group with the same goal.

Your personal vision can also play into your business vision. It should include who you want to be. It is important to know you, as you are, as well as who you want to become. This includes your:

- Habits
- Attitudes
- Points of view
- Values

If you are unclear about yourself, you will be unclear about your future. (And this makes it hard to be of service to others.) Because of this, the destination of your vision should be emotional, physical, spiritual, and intellectual.

Learn what you want, and the rest will fall into place from there. Ask yourself tough questions.

- Where do you want to be in five (ten, twenty) years?
- What is wealth?
- What is success?

Discover your answers. You are your best source of truth for all these situations. Latch on. Anything is possible within a vision. I'm the resource for the steps along the way.

Remember to include emotions, feelings, and senses.

Successful visions evoke big passions.

Guess what's really exciting about this? It's the fact that reality is blind to our vision. Cool thought, huh?

Reality cannot see what we see. A vision gives us the capability to see beyond our current reality, creating and inventing what does not exist right now. Then we start becoming what we are not right now but want to be. This takes place through the power of the subconscious mind. Its thoughts are very influential and guide everything in our lives!

We must craft our vision so it is undeniably important in all aspects of life – physically, emotionally, spiritually, corporately. Building a vision does not have to be difficult if we know exactly what it is we see for ourselves in the future.

Build it to a high standard of excellence. Then review it frequently until it becomes a part of you.

Now, remember that it is not about you. What? Did I read that right? I assure you, you did.

In reading the last several paragraphs, it's easy to become consumed by thinking about our own vision while forgetting about our clients' visions for their lives. This is a book about becoming a Servant Advisor™, after all.

Remember that once you've determined your life's vision, it's important to take your clients through the same process. Otherwise, why are we doing any of this?

You hold the answers to all the questions you need to resolve to create a vision and grow your life as wildly big and beautiful as you desire.

Part Four | 7 Core Tenets

"Knowledge is of no value unless you put it into practice."

- Anton Chekhov

These 7 Core Tenets are necessary for you to be a Servant Advisor.

Pay close attention and make sure you bring a lively narrative to each one and how it can pertain to your life. I can guide you with examples in a book, but through working together to see what this really looks and feels like, you can take your sincerity and desire and help it explode into something incredible, something amazing that has eluded you.

Shake things up.

Connect with a way to create a powerful shift in your heart and mind.

Basically, become more awesome by becoming a Servant Advisor. Let your actions with your clients, family, and community become your best marketing resource.

Nothing makes your visions and successes more powerful than these things. Everything will change and it'll thrill you.

It is part of the journey of the cultivation and birth of a Servant Advisor.

Core Tenet #1
Be understanding: Listen to know

Core Tenet #2
Be selfless: It's not about you

Core Tenet #3
Be accountable: You are responsible

Core Tenet #4
Be influential: Serve the highest need

Core Tenet #5
Be honorable: Integrity matters

Core Tenet #6
Be energetic: Enthusiasm is contagious

Core Tenet #7
Be focused: Ready. Aim. Serve!

If I am not doing all these practices every day in business, I am not doing my job right.

For those who may just be starting this journey, know that this does not just come together. It's not a transaction, it's a process where a plan is created based on where you are today. Then you can be guided toward effective changes that last.

Not short term.

Not occasionally.

But long-term lasting changes that are better.

It's not about being a super human, it's about being a Servant Advisor. This is the thought that should always guide us.

Tenet One
Be Understanding: Listen to Know

One of our deepest needs is to know we are heard and understood.

Put yourself in the shoes of your client or prospective client. Few people can communicate what they need or want. They may talk about their hopes for their portfolio and say they need an 8% return. Okay, that sounds good, but Servant Advisors™ must go further.

What's the need behind the need?

Why do they have to have that number?

What are their plans?

Is their level of risk one that even allows for it?

Maybe what they truly desire can be achieved with something else.

When Julie and I prepared to move from Kansas City to commit on working on our marriage, we had to consider many choices. We'd thought about getting retirement homes someday in many different areas.

Suddenly "someday" was already "today."

We had to evaluate our needs and what could and would work.

Learning to dive into these serious and somewhat intimate conversations with clients is not an easy task. The training to do it is one that is precise. Practice, feedback, and developing your own style to achieve this become important.

It takes conscious effort, but when it happens and you have the right processes to do this effectively, listening to what is really being said becomes easier.

This is when we can also listen for what is *not* being shared.

People grow up with a specific mindset around money. We have our own attitudes, beliefs, and behaviors when it comes to earning, spending, saving, and investing. Add in how a person feels about donating money or passing it on to family or charitable institutions, and it grows more complicated. Now there is this mix of feelings that, at times, can be quite daunting.

Experiences have proven one thing to me. No matter where a person or a couple is on their financial path, seldom do they feel they have enough or will *ever* have enough. Many have fears, often unexpressed, that dampens their spirit and resolve.

A Servant Advisor's ability to listen and discover where peoples' fears, thoughts, and goals lie on any given day is critical. It helps us cement our relationship with clients. When we do this, we can receive incredible fulfillment beyond any transaction, fee, or commission.

I get such joy out of showing Advisors how they can become a part of peoples' stories and use what they learn as a foundation to build clients' lives in an incredible manner – in ways that extend far beyond money alone.

As for you, be fearless in giving freely of your knowledge, skills, and expertise. Earn their trust!

Act! Build your dream practice by:

1. Improving your listening skills,
2. Developing an acute degree of empathy, and
3. Sharing an optimistic view of what can be achieved.

Final thought…

You Advisors who have some level of shame from past mistakes need to realize today is a new day. Take advantage of the tools, resources, coaching, and learning available so you can use this step (as it is action) to develop your "2.0" version – better and sustainable.

Create a new experience for clients!

Tenet Two
Be Selfless: It's Not About You

The key to this practice is to know when to respond, i.e., in the moment or later.

When we interact with our clients, they are not there to hear our story. We are there to hear their story; that is the story that matters.

By focusing on helping them, a strong relationship is developed.

Sure, you'll share a little bit and have some banter at first – the "niceties." And that is fun and enjoyable, because the human experience is meant to be. It must be this way if you're a Servant Advisor™.

Then the more serious topics begin. This is where the distinction begins. We must position the conversation by getting down to needs, then the solutions. It's a selfless approach.

A recent Advisor I was coaching started telling me his plan for listening and engagement. He said he could get clients to sign up for a membership and that would give him more leads.

After a big WHOA and bigger STOP, I said, "Okay, what are you doing for the people who pay money to join this club? What are you doing to help those people? What's the benefit to them?"

He answered that they get access to him, it's a networking group. That's about where he left it.

NOTE: This Advisor's thinking isn't uncommon, and it doesn't even sound wrong on the surface, but it still misses the mark.

If we want to get referrals, our first focus must be on the needs of the people we serve. They are not coming to us so they can send us referrals; they are coming to us because they need something.

When we are selfless, we deliver value and the narrative changes. It becomes about more than prices, fees, and so on. People know they are being taken care of and that is most important. They may not say it is right away, but they do feel that way most all the time. They just want to be treated well and fairly. When we're selfless, it's easy to see we are focused on that too.

Remember, while all of us are at the center of our universe with all our hopes, dreams, visions, wishes, and desires, a Servant Advisor is, first and

112

foremost, primarily focused on the needs and wants, dreams, visions, wishes, and desires of the client or prospective client.

It doesn't matter if we are face-to-face or voice-to-voice, our ability to take a back seat will ultimately determine how high we climb.

Asking questions, listening attentively, nodding in understanding, taking notes, and responding appropriately will serve our client.

Prospective clients come into our world because of what we are expected to do for them.

Client relationships endure and last because of who we are and what we stand for.

When we shine a light on what others need and want in all areas of our life and work, we build trust, develop respect, and at the heart of the matter, we honor others.

By doing this well and developing a personal philosophy of putting others first, it will lead to two specific results including, but not limited to, (1) a relationship for life, and (2) an endless stream of referrals.

Would you like this?

Act! Build your dream practice by:

1. Developing a set of open-ended questions,
2. Taking copious notes, and
3. Creating a set of prioritized action steps.

Many advisors do this well, and with a limited number of client interactions. However, when we build a relationship, we should always be glad to hear from our clients – they are placing trust in us, after all.

By making this practice universal, it strengthens the foundation and sets the stage for unlimited growth. Get started at www.theservantadvisor.com.

Tenet Three
Be Accountable: You Are Responsible

Somehow it has become fashionable for people to point the finger at others for their own mistakes and missteps. It's an ugly trend, a combination of laziness and the desire to hide our humanness.

This type of bad behavior plays out at the highest levels of leadership in government, business, religion, sports, and education. When we do witness or experience someone taking responsibility, it feels strange – way too unfamiliar. What a breath of fresh air! This is called accountability and, unfortunately, it is lacking, which is putting future generations at risk of not understanding this important concept.

As an Advisor, we are accountable for everything from waking up at a certain time to getting into the office at a certain time, being on time for an appointment, and bringing our best skills forth at any meetings we have.

All this responsibility lies with us.

We need to understand why it is so important.

All of us should make our habit one of accountability and responsibility – always.

Everything we touch is something we are responsible for.

Things do grow complicated as we grow our business. We could end up with hundreds of clients, and each one deserves 100% accountability from us.

How do we manage that while keeping our joy and sanity?

We learn how to do things right the first time.

Cutting corners with clients due to our schedule or workload is something we never do if we're a Servant Advisor™. We get it done.

Now, I would suggest that you need to have a system in place to help you get it done more effectively. Finding this system is one of the best growth policies I have with my clients.

**"Remind yourself each and every day,
that if it is to be, it is up to me."**

This quote by William H. Johnsen is a beacon to remind you of this all day, every day. It will elevate your stature in the minds of your clients and in your marketplace.

Also note: *There is a distinct difference between a reason and an excuse.*

There can always be a reason, often beyond our control or caused by external circumstances, that prevents us from performing at our best on any given day or with any given relationship. Living in this land of excuses is no way to grow a business or become a better, stronger, more capable person.

Act! Build your dream practice by:

1. Keeping your commitments;
2. Managing your resources, including time and energy; and
3. Acknowledging your mistakes when they happen.

A Servant Advisor is accountable when he or she takes ultimate responsibility for what they do and can provide a satisfactory reason for the success or failure of their intentions and actions.

Tenet Four
Be Influential: Serve the Highest Need

Using influence for the right reasons is always going to be selfless and serve a client's needs best. It's a priority we cannot waver on.

To me, influence is analogous to "sales." It's the broader perspective of the concept. Many people also think negatively of salespeople, associating them with all the qualities that are the opposite of the principles discussed here.

How can we go from people looking at us as a salesperson to viewing us as a participant in their biggest decisions? Influence!

Most people resist doing what they are told to do. Influence must come into play and it must serve someone's best interests if they are going to be open to it. This is simple to say, and even to understand, yet more challenging to do.

Helping people see what's best for them on their own is influence.

The other side of influence is identifying those who have been a positive influence in our life – guiding us and not just telling us what to do. We must make a commitment to never lose touch with who we are and our life experiences, because they do define us.

Look at where you are today, compared to where you came from. I am certain you could create a list of people who have had influence on your life and business. Maybe it was your mother or father, a teacher, coach, or early employer. Who has been influential in helping you become who you are?

Give these people the honor and credit they deserve. They are not expecting it, but to show you've taken note is meaningful.

When it comes to people who have had the largest influence on our lives, we often do not realize the scope of their influence until they're in our rearview mirror. We can consider ourselves fortunate if we have even two or three individuals of influence in our life today. This is wealth.

Real influence comes when a person believes in us with no thought of gain. He or she sees something in us that we often cannot see.

While these people of influence in our life are treasures, we also must think about who we can lift up and show they mean something to us.

Maybe it's a heartfelt thank you that makes all the difference.

Perhaps it is a tribute to another in some capacity, a story or a speech for an event they have going on.

Influence is beautiful when it is used for good.

Act! Build your dream practice by:

1. Making a list of your influencers;
2. Making a list of people you believe in; and
3. When possible, look for ways to communicate your gratitude and belief.

A Servant Advisor™ makes influence a best practice every day. When we own a mindset of everlasting gratitude and uplifting belief, we can take our success to the highest levels.

Tenet Five
Be Honorable: Integrity Matters

There are two types of integrity:

1. Integrity of your word
2. Integrity of your work

You cannot be a Servant Advisor™ without a high-quality level of work.

A Servant Advisor must have integrity when it comes to their word. When we say we're going to do something, we do it. If it's returning a call within 24 hours, we get it done no matter what. Hundreds and hundreds of clients always received a phone call back from me within 24 hours. (Yes, I can get this done without sacrificing anything due to the efficient systems I've created.)

Companies must learn the right systems to have in place to make this a necessity for all their Advisors. This type of training starts with a change of mindset for established Advisors and goes all the way into hiring those who understand integrity.

Loyalty in a business culture and with clients is built from integrity in our word and work. They cannot be separated out from each other.

Also...we may want to "do it all alone," but in reality, no one accomplishes anything great alone.

At the core of every quality relationship, respect, trust, and honor exist. When we try to live by these qualities, good things happen. Are we going to be perfect? No. There are no perfect people; we all make mistakes. What happens during these moments is what defines us.

When a client or relationship goes awry, the source of its demise often comes down to a lack of honor. Something has taken place that made a person feel their business or relationship with you was taken for granted, perhaps not appreciated.

Good intentions are not enough.
Our thoughts, words, ideas, and actions
must still go through an *honor* filter.

How we communicate is as important as what we communicate. When and where we communicate with others can impact the degree of honor we have for another human being.

In what ways have you been honored over the course of your career? Who honored you? How did it feel? Can you describe it? Honor leaves clues.

By dissecting moments of honor, we can look for ways to replicate it in others. And when this exists, so too can respect and trust.

Act! Build your dream practice by:

1. Creating an honor journal (a list of those who have honored you);
2. Describing in detail how you have been honored; and
3. Repeating the process with people in your life – honoring others.

A Servant Advisor is honorable in thoughts, words, actions, and deeds. When we put another person's well-being above ours, we will always act with integrity. Honor protects us from our human shortcomings. Our ROI, or "return on integrity," may be our greatest asset.

Tenet Six
Be Enthusiastic: Energy is Contagious

As Ralph Waldo Emerson said: "Nothing great was ever achieved without enthusiasm." I do not know a successful person who is not enthusiastic about what they have done, what they are doing, or what is yet to come. It's obvious.

I recall a time in my career when I was more energetic than ever to get out of bed every single morning. I couldn't wait! It was when I was an Advisor.

I've loved my other roles as well, but nothing was ever as fulfilling as being an Advisor.

Not everyone may be like me, but to give you an idea:

I loved waking up and having 10 meetings on the calendar for clients, and no matter what I did, no matter how much money I made, the most enthusiastic I ever was is linked to when I was an Advisor.

How often have you heard, *if you fail to plan, you will plan to fail*? Most people associate this with business, and it is true. However, it is also tied to energy and enthusiasm.

All of us require an energy plan. It may be even more important than a business plan.

What?! Why? Energy is to enthusiasm what a vision is to your destination.

How energetic do you feel daily? Do you wake up each morning ready to serve? Or, do you wake up with a heavy heart and a burdened mind? Your intention in this space matters.

The heavy heart and burdened mind are often a result of lost direction or of not bringing out the fulfillment in your opportunity as an Advisor.

Consider this…

When you look forward to a meeting or when a client or prospective client looks forward to meeting with you, a significant hurdle is conquered.

Thankfully, energy can be created, and it is sustainable. To do this requires simple, deliberate decisions and actions.

A Servant Advisor™ makes the right choice more often than the wrong choice. Do the right thing.

Act! Build your dream practice by:

1. Creating an energy plan;
2. Grounding your day with energy practices; and
3. Making course corrections in real time.

A Servant Advisor is upbeat, energetic, and optimistic. Our momentum is often dependent on our degree of energy. If we take our energy for granted, we can kiss our momentum good-bye.

Tenet Seven
Be Focused: Ready. Aim. Serve!

If you ask a group of Advisors who would like to have better focus daily, nearly all hands will go up. We don't always know how to define focus; however, we know what it feels like to be out of focus or off-track.

Focus allows us a way to make decisions easier and to maintain the discipline to see what we start through to completion.

The more focused we are, the easier everything becomes. At the end of the day, when we put our head on our pillow and have our moment of truth, ask, "Did I make the most out of this day, or did I allow everyone and anything to get in my way?"

Success is not about working hard, it's about working smart. Everyone benefits from our good work ethic and commitment to our craft.

There will always be a call, an email, a problem in life. When we easily lose focus, we get derailed. It happens! It's in the bouncing back that we regain control. The quicker we can rebound from anything, the more we increase our odds of building a strong foundation for our success.

Act! Build your dream practice by:

1. Deciding what you want;
2. Creating a visual reminder of what matters; and
3. Eliminating the gray areas in your life and work.

We tend to get what we focus on and www.theservantadvisor.com is a tool to help Advisors become Servant Advisors™, armed with strategies to succeed. This helps to define in detail what matters and grounds his or her day in the highest-value activities.

Are You The Next Servant Advisor™?

"The best way to find yourself is to lose yourself in the service of others."

- Mahatma Gandhi

You've just read something that has given you options with the potential to change your life and the lives of others.

A brief understanding of how every experience in your life is one that can help make you a stronger Advisor has been revealed.

Visions have been discussed in detail. What does yours tell you? Are you meant to be all in as a Servant Advisor™, or mediocre and unchallenged? You are meant to be challenged, coached for growth and better success.

Most Advisors spend endless hours thinking about ways to rapidly accelerate their success. They look outward and attend events, take seminars, and so on. What they fail to do is work with people who help them look inward.

This is where I come in.

Servant Advisors are now starting to enter the financial services arena. They are changing the narrative and game in their area. It's powerful and clients' needs are being met.

I know some of you were curious to see what the entire Servant Advisor thing was about. Is it something that could be of benefit? Contact me to find out. Let's talk.

It begins here: www.theservantadvisor.com.

I am grateful to you for reading this book.

Thank you for showing interest in shifting the way Advisors do their work and help clients.

There's a lot to cover and, like I'd promised at the beginning of this book, I wanted to keep it simple. You received good wisdom, but not everything. Piecing it all together is a bit trickier, as I am sure you have imagined.

I really do hope you consider becoming a Servant Advisor. There are no downsides to this, and you can become a pillar in your community for bringing true servanthood into the financial arena.

Everything could change for the better!

We've all got a story to share and we're all creating one with each day we wake up and go out into the world. As Advisors, it's time to take a direction in which our clients are the shining stars.

Carpe Diem. No limits.

Kris Bonocore

The Need for the
Best Advisor Network

When the vision for Best Advisor Network (BAN) first took shape in my mind, I saw a name that would represent a cultural mindset, focused specifically around Advisors throughout the United States. Perhaps even further someday. All that has gone into the formation of this concept stems from this.

Through education, resources, and a greater understanding of clients' best needs, we can offer client-centric Advisor opportunities to carry out our mission.

Our mission is to enable Advisors to fully develop their skills and expand their knowledge in all areas of their job function so they may best serve their clients.

As we reach toward this great and worthy task, BAN's overarching philosophy is Servant Advisorship™, a term that is the pulse of our aspirations. A Servant Advisor™ demonstrates:

- Understanding
- Selflessness

- Accountability
- Influence
- Integrity
- Energy
- Focus

These attributes have always been in demand, and perhaps more than ever in today's world. Most American jobs are in the service sector, and although BAN is beginning with those in the financial services industry as its foundation, it will eventually open to all who are an Advisor. We view an Advisor as any person who informs their customers on the best course of action and then helps them to execute on that action. This human factor is high value. It is meaningful in this age of technology, as ultimately, it's the connection between service provider and client that remains most relevant.

Advisor-client interactions can no longer be simply transactional; the Advisor needs to provide key information as well as an outstanding, well-rounded customer experience.

For example, Advisors in the financial services space must be able to act like a salesperson, think like an auditor, and establish trust like a confidante. Together, we can achieve this.

This may seem like a massive undertaking, and in some ways it is, but we believe in the vision and know the need for it.

About Kristopher Bonocore

Kristopher Bonocore is a driven visionary, focused on enhancing the dynamics of the Advisor/client relationship through the concept of the Servant Advisor™. In his nearly 20 years of financial services experience he has taken on many roles, including the areas of leadership, training, and Advisor. This insight into all these areas is what fueled his strong passion for the company's vision and gives him the drive and ability to bring it to life. He enjoys setting the bar for his peers and for those on his team with a client-first approach.

Now he is taking his years of proven experience and is forming a new option for those Advisors who want to become game-changers in the lives of their clients by becoming Servant Advisors. According to Kris, "This is the way to cultivate a win/win relationship with clients. Their needs must be met first and the rest will fall into place."

To start this initiative, options exist for Advisors that are new, fresh, and innovative in their approach and implementation.

The areas of specialty for the umbrella company of Kris's new venture, Best Advisor Network, will connect with Advisors who wish to:

- Be coached in becoming a Servant Advisor;
- Immerse themselves in a network of Servant Advisors to receive support and camaraderie to develop better client service and personal practices; and/or
- Open their own financial business that is modeled off Kris's Servant Advisorship™ practices and leadership model.

As part of his outreach, Kris encourages people to connect with the Best Advisor Network at www.theservantadvisor.com.

Acknowledgements

Many thanks to the countless and invaluable people who made the vision of writing a book become reality. There are so many of you who mean so much to me, including a vast and diverse group of friends, family, business associates, and mentors who have influenced and supported me over the years. All of you were there for me then and you remain at my side now as my journey continues.

Within this vast group, I'd like to give special acknowledgement to Julie, Madison, Ethan, Erik, Jayme, David, John, Tom, Michael, Chris, Sam, Darius, Alex, Matt, Nick, Ted, Paul, Doug, Steve, Brian, Josh, and Ray. Your contributions to my life and my career have been invaluable.

Also, thank you to all my friends and former colleagues at Financial Engines and The Mutual Fund Store. I loved every minute of our time together. Your collective and tireless work toward a common vision inspired me and gave me pure joy to wake up to each day as I rushed off to work.

Thank you to all my former clients for their trust and confidence. Without you, there would be little to speak of.

Thank you to all Advisors in the industry. The work you do is vital to the future of our society. The world needs more of you who are sincerely devoted to serving clients.

Contact Best Advisor Network

www.theservantadvisor.com
theservantadvisor@gmail.com

Appendix

"Good artists copy; great artists steal."

- Pablo Picasso

The following pages include a series of ideas, philosophies, and illustrations. Over the years, I've learned them, spoken about them, taught them, employed them, and evolved with them. Some of them help to bring the book's concepts to life and some help bring you to life.

Not all concepts are mine, although there are few new notions under the sun and too many existing notions that need further promotion. The fundamentals of each are captured but offer much to be expanded upon in discussion, in thought, and in practice.

Let's spend some time expanding on these in ways that can help us serve clients and pursue excellence, together...

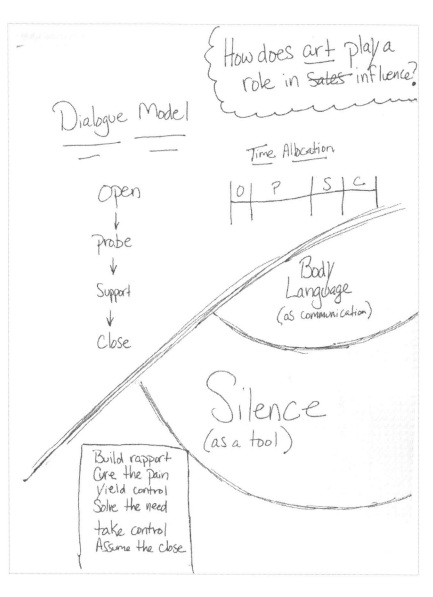

How does art play a role in Sales influence?

Dialogue Model

Open
↓
Probe
↓
Support
↓
Close

Time Allocation

| O | P | | S | C |

Body Language
(as communication)

Silence
(as a tool)

Build rapport
Cure the pain
Yield control
Solve the need
take control
Assume the close

www.theservantadvisor.com

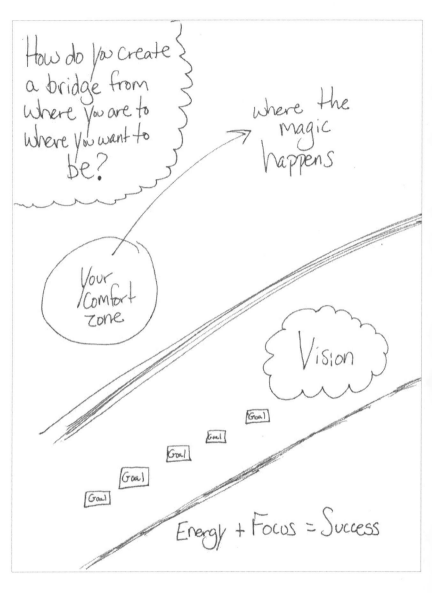

Client Reviews

How do you deliver an experience they cannot receive anywhere else?

→ frequency
→ Scheduling
→ experience
→ actionable next steps
→ Continuation

Topics

- insurance
- goal plan
- will
- trust
- Children
- budget
- inheritance
- family
- investments

Strategic Partnerships

{ Who are your business partners?

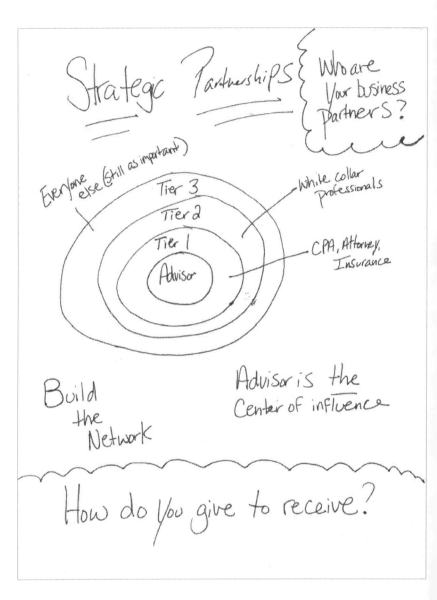

Everyone else (Still as important)

Tier 3
Tier 2
Tier 1
Advisor

White collar professionals

CPA, Attorney, Insurance

Build the Network

Advisor is the Center of influence

How do you give to receive?

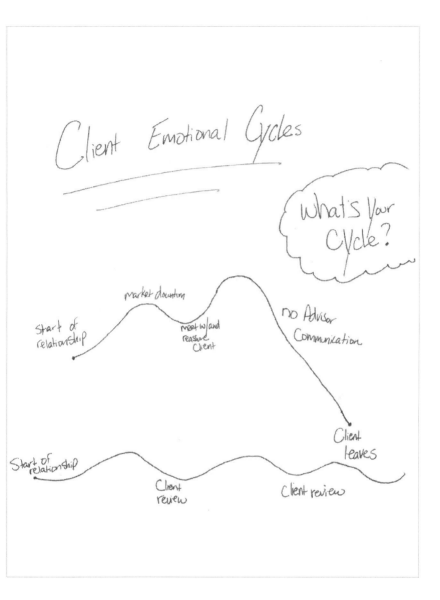

Client Emotional Cycles

What's Your Cycle?

Start of relationship

market downturn

meet w/and reassure Client

no Advisor Communication

Client leaves

Start of relationship

Client review

Client review

www.theservantadvisor.com

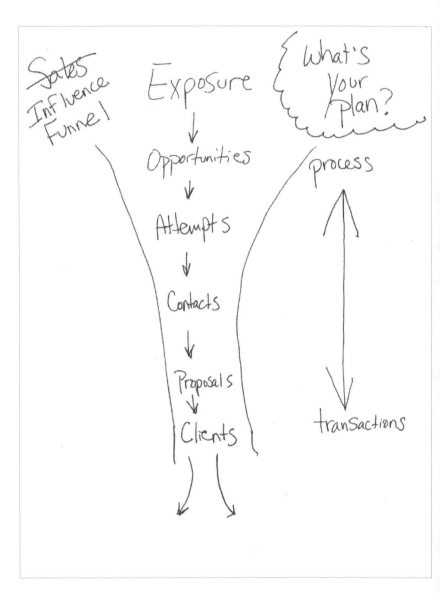

Sales Influence Funnel

Exposure
↓
Opportunities
↓
Attempts
↓
Contacts
↓
Proposals
↓
Clients

What's your plan?

process

transactions

Made in the USA
Monee, IL
22 February 2020